Wok Wonders

With
Debra Murray

Acknowledgements

This cookbook took the efforts of many talented people, without them, I would not have been able to make this book a reality.

First, I would like to thank my husband Martin and my daughter Nevar. Their love and patience, inspire me to create these recipes. I want to thank my parents and my sister Gail for such a wonderful childhood, they are the best friends in the world.

My sincere gratitude to Chef Wolfgang Puck, I cannot thank you enough for this wonderful career and letting me share the set with you. Thank you for the laughter, I adore you as a chef and a person. I continue to be amazed and inspired by you.

A special thanks to Jonathan Schwartz for making these books. I want to thank Sydney Silverman and Mike Sanseverino, they are the nicest people one could work for.

I want to thank all the incredible HSN viewers who have embraced my books. Your support has been overwhelming and for that I am ever grateful.

I am so lucky to have a remarkable book staff. Daniel Koren for being so patient and having such incredible skills to make these books so amazing. Christina Chancey, for your brilliant food styling and recipe testing. Chris Davis and his assistant Erica for the food photography as well as Nevar Murray and Tracy Ferguson for their art direction. I would be remiss if I did not thank Marian Getz for all the wonderful things she teaches me as well as my makeup artists Julie and Ginny.

Debra Murray

Introduction

Those familiar with my Santa Monica, California, restaurant Chinois on Main know I am very passionate about Asian cuisine. The inspiration for Chinois came from Southern California's Asian population. I wanted to bring together the flavors of Los Angeles' Koreatown, Chinatown, and Thai Town in one multicultural kitchen. Dining at Chinois, one can watch chefs create Asian-inspired dishes in large woks, tossing together the freshest and most colorful ingredients.

The wok is essential for making quickly cooked meals. The bowl shaped pan is designed to cook rapidly with little fat. Its large, fluted sides and small base allow tossing food with little effort.

Debra Murray also loves the wok. In the ten years that she has been my assistant at the Home Shopping Network, I have witnessed her passion for good cooking and quality appliances. The wok is one of her favorites. Debra is not just a talented cook but her creativity allows her to take greater advantage of the wok. Along with classic Asian dishes like Beef Teriyaki and Orange Sesame Pork, you will find unexpected recipes like Bourbon BBQ Fondue, Dynamic Steakhouse Onion Rings, Pasta Primavera, and desserts such as Marshmallow Cereal Treats, White Chocolate Fondue, and Old Fashioned Candy Apples. The wok may not have been intended for these dishes, but it turns out it's perfect for them. This collection of recipes and a high quality wok will enable you to make delicious and effortless meals.

Wolfgang Puck

Table Of Contents

Fabulous Frying
Page 8

Fondues & Hot Pot
For Social Gatherings
Page 39

Sensational Soups
Page 52

Table Of Contents

Wok Tips

There are a few wok tips I would like to share with you to help you achieve excellent results:

- The best way to cook stir-fry is to set up all the ingredients ahead of time and place them within reach of the wok. This will allow you to cook quickly without having to look for ingredients.

- For deep frying, I typically use canola oil because it has a higher smoking point, holds up longer and does not affect the taste of the food. In some recipes, I list peanut oil as an ingredient. Peanut oil truly enriches the flavor of food. However, it is more expensive and some people are experiencing food allergies to peanuts. If you prefer canola oil, feel free to substitute it for peanut oil.

- A candy thermometer is an essential tool for many of the recipes in this book. Measuring exact temperatures is critical to the success of those recipes. Place the probe in the center of the wok without touching the bottom. I suggest using a thermometer with a long probe as the wok's deep shape makes it harder to measure with a short probe.

- When preparing a candy recipe, pay close attention to the sugar mixture as it hardens quickly.

- Candy clean up is made simple by adding water to the wok and setting it to MEDIUM. The sugar will dissolve easily in the boiling liquid. You can even soak your cooking utensils in the liquid.

- I mention parchment paper frequently throughout this book. I think it does a terrific job in making clean up easier. You may choose to skip the use of parchment paper as long as you provide a stick resistant surface.

The recipes in this book were created using the revolutionary Multi Purpose Deluxe Electric Wok by Wolfgang Puck. However, the recipes can be used in conjunction with any wok. If you own the original Wolfgang Puck wok or any other wok, use this chart to make the necessary conversions:

Multi Purpose Deluxe Electric Wok by Wolfgang Puck	Original Wok By Wolfgang Puck	Temperature Equivalent (Degrees Fahrenheit)
KEEP WARM	1 - 2	110°
MEDIUM	3 - 4	215°
HIGH	5 - 6	320°
SEAR	7	425°

Fabulous Frying

Crunchy Curry Shrimp

Makes 2 to 4 servings

Ingredients:

½ cup cornstarch

1 large egg, beaten

1 cup flour

1 teaspoon curry powder

1½ cups peanut oil

1 pound medium shrimp, peeled and deveined

½ cup mayonnaise

¼ cup sweet Thai chili sauce

1. Place cornstarch into a large zipper bag.
2. Pour egg into a bowl.
3. Combine flour and curry powder into a separate zipper bag.
4. Pour oil into wok and set to SEAR.
5. Place shrimp into the zipper bag with cornstarch; shake well.
6. Dip shrimp into egg and place into zipper bag with flour; shake well.
7. Add 5 shrimp to wok; cook for 3 minutes on each side.
8. Remove shrimp and place on paper towels to drain excess oil.
9. Repeat with remaining shrimp.
10. In a large bowl, combine mayonnaise and chili sauce.
11. Toss shrimp in sauce and serve.

Deb's Tip:
Serve on a bed of lettuce and top with chopped green onions.

Worth The Work Fries

Makes 2 servings

Ingredients:

1½ cups peanut oil

2 large russet potatoes, peeled

½ teaspoon salt

1. Wash and cut potatoes to desired shape.
2. Pat dry using paper towels.
3. Pour oil into wok and set to SEAR.
4. Using a candy thermometer, measure oil temperature until it reaches 325 degrees.
5. Add half the potatoes to wok; cook for 4 minutes.
6. Using a skimmer, remove fries and place them on paper towels.
7. Repeat with remaining fries.
8. Using a candy thermometer, measure oil temperature until it reaches 375 degrees.
9. Add half the fries into the wok; cook for 3 additional minutes or until desired doneness.
10. Repeat with remaining fries.
11. Season fries immediately with salt and serve.

Deb's Tip:
For added flavor, sprinkle fries with malt vinegar before serving.

Meat Pies

Ingredients:

½ cup prepared mashed potatoes

½ pound ground beef

1 small onion, chopped

2 teaspoons salt

½ teaspoon freshly ground pepper

¼ cup frozen peas and carrots

1 can (16.3 ounces) Pop N' Fresh biscuit dough

1½ cups canola oil

1. Set wok to SEAR and add beef.
2. Break up beef into small pieces using a wooden spoon and cook through; drain fat and place beef back into the wok.
3. Add onions, salt and pepper to wok; cook for 2 minutes.
4. Add peas and carrots to wok; cover and cook for 2 minutes.
5. In a bowl, combine mashed potatoes and meat mixture; mix well.
6. Stretch each biscuit into a 5-inch circle.
7. Place a tablespoon of meat mixture on ½ the biscuit circle.
8. Pull the dough from the opposite half over the meat mixture forming a half moon; press edges to seal.
9. Clean wok, pour oil into wok and set to SEAR.
10. Using a candy thermometer, measure oil temperature until it reaches 325 degrees.
11. Add 2 meat pies to wok; cook for 2 minutes on each side.
12. Remove meat pies and place on paper towels to drain excess oil.
13. Repeat with remaining meat pies and serve.

Japanese Shrimp Tempura

Makes 2 to 4 servings

Ingredients:

1 pound large shrimp, peeled and deveined

¼ cup cornstarch

1½ cups canola oil

Batter:

1 cup ice water

1 cup sifted flour

½ teaspoon salt

2 eggs, beaten

1. Add cornstarch to a large zipper bag.
2. In a bowl, combine water, flour, salt and eggs; mix well.
3. Add shrimp to bag and shake well.
4. Dip shrimp into prepared batter.
5. Pour oil into wok and set to SEAR.
6. Using a candy thermometer, measure oil temperature until it reaches 365 degrees.
7. Add 5 shrimp to wok; cook 4 minutes on each side.
8. Repeat with remaining shrimp and serve.

Deb's Tip:
This is terrific for scallops, vegetables or even chicken as well.

Crab Rangoons

Ingredients:

4 ounces cream cheese

12 fresh chives, finely chopped

½ teaspoon soy sauce

½ teaspoon hot sauce

8 ounces crab meat

1 package wonton skins

1½ cups canola oil

1. Using a food processor, soften cream cheese.
2. Add chives, soy sauce and hot sauce to food processor; mix well.
3. Gently add crab meat to mixture.
4. Place 1 teaspoon of crab mixture in the center of each wonton skin.
5. Moisten edges with water and fold skin in half to form a triangle; press edges to seal.
6. Pull the bottom corners of the triangle down and overlap slightly; moisten corner with water and press to seal.
7. Pour oil into wok and set to SEAR.
8. Using a candy thermometer, measure oil temperature until it reaches 350 degrees.
9. Add 5 wontons to wok; cook for 4 minutes until golden brown.
10. Remove wontons and place on paper towels to drain excess oil.
11. Repeat with remaining wontons and serve.

Deb's Tip:
Combine a tablespoon of chili garlic sauce, a teaspoon of soy sauce and a half cup of raspberry preserves to make a perfect dipping sauce.

Far East Chicken Wings

Ingredients:

2 pounds chicken wings

1½ cups canola oil

2 tablespoons salted butter

2 tablespoons hot sauce

2 tablespoons honey

1 tablespoon hoisin sauce

1 tablespoon sesame seeds

1. Wash and pat dry wings.
2. Pour oil into wok and set to SEAR.
3. Using a candy thermometer, measure oil temperature until it reaches 375 degrees.
4. Add 6 wings to wok; cook for 5 minutes on each side.
5. Repeat with remaining wings.
6. In a saucepan on medium heat, melt butter and add hot sauce, honey and hoisin sauce.
7. Toss wings in sauce, sprinkle with sesame seeds and serve.

Yummy Chicken Nuggets

Ingredients:

1 large egg, beaten

1 box seasoned coating mix for chicken

1 pound boneless, skinless chicken breast, cut into 1-inch cubes

1½ cups peanut oil

1. Add egg to a bowl and spread coating mix on a plate.
2. Dip chicken in egg and roll in coating.
3. Pour oil into wok and set to SEAR.
4. Using a candy thermometer, measure oil temperature until it reaches 350 degrees.
5. Add 6 pieces of chicken to wok; cook for 2 minutes on each side.
6. Remove chicken and place on paper towels to drain excess oil.
7. Repeat with remaining chicken and serve.

Dynamic Steakhouse Onion Rings

Ingredients:

1 jumbo sweet onion, thinly sliced

1 cup water

1 cup all-purpose flour

1 teaspoon salt

½ teaspoon cayenne pepper

1 large egg, beaten

1 cup breadcrumbs

1½ cups peanut oil

1. Soak onions in water.
2. In a bowl, combine flour, salt and pepper; mix well.
3. Remove onions from water and shake off excess water.
4. Toss onions in flour mixture and shake off excess flour.
5. Pour egg into a bowl.
6. Spread breadcrumbs on a plate.
7. Dip onions in egg and roll in breadcrumbs; shake off excess.
8. Pour oil into wok and set to SEAR.
9. Using a candy thermometer, measure oil temperature until it reaches 375 degrees.
10. Add 5 onions slices to wok; cook for 2 minutes on each side.
11. Remove onions and place on paper towels to drain excess oil.
12. Sprinkle onions with salt while still warm.
13. Repeat with remaining onions.

Deb's Tip:
Serve with a juicy steak and a baked potato.

Sweet Potato French Fries

Ingredients:

2 large sweet potatoes, peeled

1½ cups peanut oil

1 teaspoon salt

1. Wash and cut potatoes to desired shape.
2. Pat dry potatoes using paper towels.
3. Pour oil into wok and set to SEAR.
4. Using a candy thermometer, measure oil temperature until it reaches 350 degrees.
5. Add half the french fries to wok, cook for 2 minutes on each side.
6. Remove fries and place on paper towels to drain excess fat.
7. Sprinkle fries with salt while still hot.
8. Repeat with remaining fries and serve.

Deb's Tip:
Try steak seasoning instead of salt on these french fries.

Bacon Wrapped Shrimp

Ingredients:

1 pound jumbo shrimp, butterflied

1 tablespoon horseradish

8 slices bacon, cut in half

Toothpicks

1 cup canola oil

1. Fill each shrimp with ¼ teaspoon horseradish.
2. Wrap each shrimp in bacon and secure with a toothpick.
3. Pour oil into wok and set to SEAR.
4. Using a candy thermometer, measure oil temperature until it reaches 375 degrees.
5. Add 3 shrimp to wok; cook for 3 minutes on each side.
6. Remove shrimp and place on paper towels to drain excess fat.
7. Repeat with remaining shrimp and serve.

Deb's Tip:
Combine fresh horseradish with Thousand Island dressing to make an amazing dipping sauce.

Beer Battered Fish Fry

Makes 2 to 4 servings

Ingredients:

½ cup flour

1 large egg, separated

1 teaspoon canola oil

1 teaspoon seasoning salt

½ cup beer, room temperature

1½ cups peanut oil

1 pound cod, cut into 1-inch strips

1. In a bowl, combine flour, egg yolk, canola oil, salt and beer; mix well.
2. Cover bowl and refrigerate for 2 hours.
3. In a separate bowl, beat egg white until stiff.
4. Fold egg white into the refrigerated batter.
5. Pour peanut oil into wok and set to SEAR.
6. Using a candy thermometer, measure oil temperature until it reaches 350 degrees.
7. Dip cod strips in batter.
8. Add 2 cod strips to wok; cook for 4 minutes on each side.
9. Remove cod and place on paper towels to drain excess oil.
10. Repeat with remaining cod and serve.

Deb's Tip:
This batter also works great on vegetables, chicken and seafood.

Coconut Shrimp

Ingredients:

1 pound extra large shrimp, peeled and deveined

½ cup cornstarch

2 tablespoons seltzer water

¾ cup flour

1 teaspoon curry powder

¾ teaspoon baking powder

¼ teaspoon salt

1 large egg, beaten

2 cups unsweetened coconut flakes

1½ cups canola oil

Dipping Sauce:

½ cup orange marmalade

2 tablespoons sweet chili sauce

1. Place cornstarch in a large zipper bag.
2. Place shrimp in the bag and shake until completely coated.
3. In a bowl, combine seltzer water, flour, curry powder, baking powder, salt and egg; do not over-mix, it should still be lumpy.
4. Let batter rest for 15 minutes.
5. Pour oil into wok and set to SEAR.
6. Using a candy thermometer, measure oil temperature until it reaches 350 degrees.
7. Spread coconut flakes on a plate.
8. Dip shrimp in batter and roll in coconut flakes.
9. Add 3 shrimp to wok; cook for 3 minutes on each side.
10. Repeat with remaining shrimp.
11. In a bowl, combine dipping sauce ingredients.
12. Serve shrimp with dipping sauce.

Italian Wontons

Ingredients:

6 ounces sweet Italian sausage, casing removed

¼ cup onions, chopped

1 small red bell pepper, finely chopped

1 tablespoon fresh parsley, chopped

½ teaspoon garlic powder

½ cup Mozzarella cheese, shredded

¼ cup Parmesan cheese, grated

1 package wonton skins

1½ cups canola oil

1 cup marinara sauce

1. Place sausage into wok and set to SEAR.
2. Break up sausage into small pieces using a wooden spoon and cook through; drain fat and place sausage back into the wok.
3. Add onions, peppers, parsley and garlic powder to wok; cook for 3 minutes.
4. Transfer sausage mixture to a bowl and add cheeses; mix well.
5. Clean wok, pour oil into the wok and set to SEAR.
6. Using a candy thermometer, measure oil temperature until it reaches 350 degrees.
7. Place wonton skins on a flat surface with one corner towards you like a diamond.
8. Place 1 teaspoon of sausage mixture in the center of each wonton.
9. Moisten the wonton edges with water and fold one corner over to form a triangle; press to seal.
10. Bring the two points to the center of the wonton and press down with moist fingers.
11. Cover with a damp paper towel until ready to cook.
12. Add 3 wontons to wok; cook for 3 minutes on each side until golden brown.
13. Remove wontons and place on paper towels to drain excess oil.
14. Repeat with remaining wontons.
15. Serve with marinara sauce.

Easy Egg Rolls

Ingredients:

1½ cups shredded coleslaw mix without dressing

1 small onion, chopped

¾ cup chicken, cooked and diced

1 tablespoon teriyaki sauce

6 egg roll skins

1½ cups canola oil

1. In a bowl, combine coleslaw, onions, chicken and teriyaki sauce.
2. Place egg roll skin on a flat surface with one corner towards you like a diamond.
3. Place ½ cup of mixture in the center of each egg roll skin.
4. Take the lower corner of the egg roll skin and roll up, folding in the sides at the same time.
5. Moisten edges with water and press to seal.
6. Pour oil into wok and set to SEAR.
7. Using a candy thermometer, measure oil temperature until it reaches 350 degrees.
8. Add 2 rolls to wok; cook for two minutes on each side.
9. Remove rolls and place on paper towels to drain excess oil.
10. Repeat with remaining rolls and serve.

Deb's Tip:
For a twist, substitute cooked pork or shrimp for the chicken.

Panko Scallops

Ingredients:

1 pound sea scallops
½ cup cornstarch
1 large egg, beaten
2 cups panko breadcrumbs
1½ cups peanut oil
½ teaspoon salt

1. Wash and pat dry scallops with paper towels.
2. Place cornstarch into a large zipper bag.
3. Add egg to a bowl.
4. Spread panko on a plate.
5. Place scallops into zipper bag; shake well.
6. Dip scallops into egg mixture and roll in panko.
7. Pour oil into wok and set to SEAR.
8. Using a candy thermometer, measure oil temperature until it reaches 350 degrees.
9. Add 5 scallops to wok; cook for 3 minutes on each side.
10. Remove scallops and place on paper towels to drain excess oil.
11. Repeat with remaining scallops.
12. Season with salt while hot and serve.

Cannoli Purses

Ingredients:

1 package egg roll skins
1 cup ricotta cheese
½ cup powdered sugar
1 teaspoon vanilla
¼ cup mini chocolate chips
1½ cups canola oil

1. Place egg roll skins on a flat surface.
2. Using a drinking glass with a 3-inch diameter, cut out circles.
3. In a bowl, combine cheese, sugar, vanilla and chocolate chips; mix well.
4. Place 1 teaspoon of cheese mixture in the center of each circle.
5. Carefully lift the edges of the circle up and press gently together to hold in place.
6. Take a 5-inch piece of string and tie a knot around each purse.
7. Pour oil into wok and set to SEAR.
8. Using a candy thermometer, measure oil temperature until it reaches 325 degrees.
9. Add 5 purses to wok; cook until golden brown.
10. Remove purses and place on paper towels to drain excess oil.
11. Repeat with remaining purses and serve.

Deb's Tip:
Dust with additional powdered sugar before serving.

Deb's Donuts

Ingredients:

1 package (8 ounces) Pop N' Fresh buttermilk biscuits

1 cup canola oil

1 container vanilla or chocolate frosting

1. Using your finger, poke a hole into the center of each biscuit.
2. Pour oil into wok and set to SEAR.
3. Using a candy thermometer, measure oil temperature until it reaches 325 degrees.
4. Add 3 biscuits to wok; cook for 3 minutes on each side.
5. Remove donuts and place on paper towels to drain excess oil.
6. Repeat with remaining donuts.
7. Open frosting container and remove seal completely.
8. Microwave frosting for 30 seconds; stir and spoon over each donut.

Deb's Tip:
For a different topping, combine a half cup of sugar and 2 teaspoons of cinnamon and dip the warm donuts into the mixture.

Fried Apple Pies

Ingredients:

1½ cups canola oil

1 can (16.3 ounces) buttermilk Pop N' Fresh biscuit dough

1 can apple pie filling

¼ cup cinnamon sugar

1. Stretch each biscuit until 5 inches in diameter.
2. Place a tablespoon of pie filling on one side of the biscuit circle.
3. Fold the dough over and crimp the edges using a fork.
4. Pour oil into wok and set to SEAR.
5. Using a candy thermometer, measure oil temperature until it reaches 325 degrees.
6. Add 1 pie to wok; cook for 4 minutes on each side.
7. Remove pie and place on paper towels to drain excess fat.
8. Sprinkle pie with cinnamon sugar.
9. Repeat with remaining pies and serve.

Fried Bananas

Ingredients:

1 package egg roll skins
8 ripe bananas
8 skewers
1½ cups canola oil
Chocolate syrup

1. Cut off the top and bottom of each banana and peel.
2. Place egg roll skin on a flat surface with one corner towards you like a diamond.
3. Place one banana on the lower corner of a skin and roll up, folding in the sides at the same time.
4. Moisten top corner with water and press to seal.
5. Insert a skewer into one end of each banana roll.
6. Pour oil into wok and set to SEAR.
7. Place 1 banana roll into wok; cook for 3 minutes on each side.
8. Repeat with remaining rolls.
9. Drizzle chocolate syrup over bananas and serve.

Deb's Tip:
For extra flavor, add your favorite jam to the rolls.

Fantastic Funnel Cake

Ingredients:

2 cups biscuit baking mix

1½ cups milk

2 tablespoons sugar

2 large eggs, beaten

1½ cups canola oil

Pastry bags

Powdered sugar

In a bowl, combine baking mix, milk, sugar and eggs; do not over-mix.

Pour batter into a pastry bag with a small hole cut at the end.

Pour oil into wok and set to SEAR.

Using a candy thermometer, measure oil temperature until it reaches 350 degrees.

Drizzle batter into the wok in a snowflake-like fashion, making sure the batter crosses over like a star.

Cook funnel cake for 1 minute on each side.

Remove funnel cake and place on paper towels to drain excess oil.

Dust with powdered sugar and serve.

Fondues & Hot Pot
For Social Gatherings

Easy Beer Cheese Fondue

Ingredients:

1 tablespoon flour

1 tablespoon extra-virgin olive oil

¾ cup beer

1 garlic clove, finely minced

8 ounces Swiss cheese, grated

4 ounces sharp Cheddar cheese, grated

1 teaspoon hot pepper sauce

1 teaspoon salt

1 teaspoon freshly ground pepper

1 large French or Italian bread, cubed

1. Add flour and oil to wok; stir to make a paste.
2. Set wok to SEAR.
3. Whisk beer into flour paste; bring to a boil.
4. Reduce wok to MEDIUM.
5. Add garlic and cheeses to wok; stir until cheeses are melted.
6. Add hot pepper sauce, salt and pepper to wok; stir.
7. Reduce wok to KEEP WARM and use as a fondue vessel.
8. Serve with bread for dipping.

Deb's Tip:
Vegetables or pretzels are great for dipping as well.

Bourbon BBQ Fondue

Makes 6 to 8 servings

Ingredients:

1 tablespoon extra-virgin olive oil

½ cup onions, chopped

4 garlic cloves, minced

½ cup tomato paste

¾ cup bourbon

2 cups ketchup

½ cup cider vinegar

3 tablespoons Worcestershire sauce

½ cup brown sugar

½ cup molasses

1 teaspoon salt

½ teaspoon freshly ground pepper

1 tablespoon mustard

1 teaspoon Louisiana hot sauce

Cocktail hotdogs

1. Pour oil into wok and set to HIGH.
2. Add onions and garlic to wok; cook for 2 minutes.
3. Add tomato paste to wok; cook for 3 minutes.
4. Add remaining ingredients, except hotdogs, to wok; cook for 20 minutes.
5. Reduce wok to KEEP WARM and use as a fondue vessel.
6. Serve with hotdogs for dipping.

Deb's Tip:
Try meatballs or chicken wings instead of hotdogs.

Cheese Fondue

Ingredients:

1½ cups dry white wine

1 garlic clove, minced

2 tablespoons kirsch

1 tablespoon cornstarch

2 cups Emmenthaler cheese, grated

2 cups Gruyere cheese, grated

1 large French or Italian bread, cubed

1. Pour wine into wok and set to SEAR; bring to a simmer.
2. Add garlic to wok.
3. In a small bowl, combine kirsch and cornstarch.
4. Whisk kirsch mixture into wok; bring to a boil.
5. Reduce wok to MEDIUM.
6. Add cheeses to wok; stir until melted.
7. Serve with bread for dipping.

Deb's Tip:
Try cooked potato slices instead of bread cubes for dipping.

Pizza Fondue

Ingredients:

1 pound lean ground beef

1 pound sweet Italian sausage, casing removed

1 medium onion, diced

2 garlic cloves, minced

1 green bell pepper, diced

8 ounces mushrooms, sliced

4 ounces pepperoni, diced

¼ cup black olives, sliced

1 teaspoon salt

½ teaspoon freshly ground pepper

1 teaspoon Italian seasoning

1 can (14½ ounces) diced tomatoes with basil and garlic

2 cups pizza sauce

Breadsticks

1. Add beef and sausage to wok and set to SEAR.
2. Break up beef and sausage into small pieces using a wooden spoon and cook through; drain fat and place beef and sausage back into the wok.
3. Add onions, garlic, peppers and mushrooms to wok; cook for 4 minutes.
4. Add remaining ingredients, except breadsticks, to wok; stir.
5. Reduce wok to MEDIUM and simmer for 10 minutes.
6. Serve with breadsticks for dipping.

Deb's Tip:
Try Mozzarella sticks or fried ravioli for dipping.

Chili Cheese Fondue

Ingredients:

1 cup heavy cream

2 cups mild Cheddar cheese, shredded

1 cup chili, homemade or canned

1 tablespoon green chiles, chopped

Tortilla chips

1. Set wok to MEDIUM.
2. Add heavy cream to wok; bring to a simmer.
3. Add cheese to wok; stir until melted.
4. Add chili and chiles to wok; stir and cook for 2 minutes.
5. Set wok to KEEP WARM and use as a serving vessel.
6. Serve with tortilla chips for dipping.

Deb's Tip:
Try using vegetables or pretzels for dipping.

Traditional Fondue

Ingredients:

2 cups flour

1 teaspoon seasoning salt

1 large egg, beaten

1 cup broccoli flowerets

1 cup cauliflower flowerets

1 chicken breast, cut into 1-inch cubes

12-inch metal skewers

1½ cups canola oil

1. In a bowl, combine flour and seasoning salt.
2. Pour egg into a separate bowl.
3. Dip broccoli, cauliflower and chicken in egg and roll in flour.
4. Put broccoli, cauliflower and chicken on skewers.
5. Pour oil into wok and set to SEAR.
6. Using a candy thermometer, measure oil temperature until it reaches 350 degrees.
7. Keep wok on SEAR and use as a fondue vessel.
8. Dip skewers into oil and cook until desired doneness.

Hot & Sour Hot Pot

Makes 6 to 8 servings

Ingredients:

2 teaspoons cornstarch

4 cups chicken stock

1 tablespoon ginger, minced

2 tablespoons cider vinegar

2 tablespoons lemon juice

1 teaspoon salt

½ teaspoon white pepper

2 green onions, chopped

For Dipping:

12-inch metal skewers

1 can (8 ounces) bamboo shoots, drained

2 cups fresh mushrooms, halved

1 pound boneless, skinless chicken breast, sliced into 1-inch strips

1 cup cauliflower flowerets

1. In a bowl, dissolve cornstarch in chicken stock and pour into wok.
2. Set wok to SEAR.
3. Add ginger, vinegar, lemon juice, salt and pepper to wok; stir and cook for 15 minutes.
4. Top broth with green onions.
5. Skewer bamboo shoots, mushrooms, chicken and cauliflower.
6. Keep wok on SEAR and use as a fondue vessel.
7. Dip skewers in hot broth and cook until desired doneness.

White Chocolate Fondue

Ingredients:

²/₃ cup heavy cream
1 bag (12 ounces) white chocolate chips
2 tablespoons brandy
Strawberries

1. Add heavy cream to wok.
2. Set wok to MEDIUM and bring to a simmer.
3. Reduce wok to KEEP WARM.
4. Add chocolate chips to wok; stir until melted.
5. Add brandy to wok; stir.
6. Use wok as a serving vessel.
7. Serve with strawberries for dipping.

Deb's Tip:
Serve with different fruits, pound cake or pretzels for dipping.

48

Chocolate Strawberry Fondue

Ingredients:

1 bag (14 ounces) caramels, unwrapped

1 bag (12 ounces) semi-sweet chocolate chips

1 can (12 ounces) evaporated milk

1 stick unsalted butter

½ cup strawberry preserves

Marshmallows

1. Add all ingredients to wok and set to MEDIUM.
2. Stir until chocolate chips and caramels are melted.
3. Reduce wok to KEEP WARM and use as a serving vessel.
4. Serve with marshmallows for dipping.

Toffee Fondue

Ingredients:

1 stick unsalted butter

1 cup light brown sugar

1 cup dark brown sugar

1 cup light corn syrup

2 tablespoons water

1 can (14 ounces) sweetened condensed milk

1 teaspoon vanilla

Sliced apples

1. Set wok to KEEP WARM.
2. Add butter to wok and let melt.
3. Increase wok to MEDIUM.
4. Add remaining ingredients, except vanilla and apples, to wok.
5. Stir continuously until sugars are dissolved and mixture thickens.
6. Add vanilla to wok; stir.
7. Reduce wok to KEEP WARM and use as a fondue vessel.
8. Serve with apples for dipping.

Deb's Tip:
Instead of apples, try pears or bananas for dipping.

Sensational Soups

Cream Of Cauliflower Soup

Ingredients:

2 tablespoons unsalted butter

1 whole shallot, minced

1 head of cauliflower, trimmed and chopped

4 cups chicken stock

1 sprig of fresh thyme

1 tablespoon fresh lemon juice

1 teaspoon salt

½ teaspoon freshly ground pepper

4 ounces cream cheese

1. Set wok to MEDIUM.
2. Add butter to wok and let melt.
3. Add shallots to wok; cook for 2 minutes.
4. Add remaining ingredients, except cream cheese, to wok; cover.
5. Increase wok to SEAR and cook for 20 minutes.
6. Remove thyme and pour soup into a blender.
7. Add cream cheese to blender and puree soup until smooth.

Tortellini Soup

Ingredients:

2 tablespoons extra-virgin olive oil

½ cup onions, diced

½ cup celery, diced

½ cup carrots, diced

1 teaspoon salt

½ teaspoon freshly ground pepper

2 tablespoons fresh parsley, chopped

4 cups chicken stock

1 can (14½ ounces) fire roasted tomatoes

1 bag (12 ounces) frozen cheese tortellini

6 basil leaves, torn

1. Pour oil into wok and set to SEAR.
2. Add onions, celery, carrots, salt and pepper to wok; cook for 2 minutes.
3. Add parsley, stock and tomatoes to wok; cover and cook for 15 minutes.
4. Add tortellini to wok; cook for 5 minutes.
5. Top with basil and serve.

Deb's Tip:
This soup is great served with fresh hot bread and pesto.

Homemade Chili

Ingredients:

1 pound lean ground beef

1 medium onion, chopped

1 can (15 ounces) dark red kidney beans

1 can (28 ounces) diced tomatoes

1 can (15 ounces) tomato sauce

1 can (4 ounces) chopped green chiles

2 tablespoons chili powder

1 teaspoon ground cumin

1 teaspoon salt

½ teaspoon freshly ground pepper

1. Set wok to SEAR and add beef.
2. Break up beef into small pieces using a wooden spoon and cook through; drain fat and place beef back into the wok.
3. Add onions to wok; cook for 2 minutes.
4. Reduce wok to MEDIUM.
5. Add remaining ingredients to wok; cook for 30 minutes.
6. Serve immediately.

Deb's Tip:
Garnish with sour cream, grated cheese and chopped green onions.

Wonton Soup

Makes 4 to 6 servings

Wontons:

1 tablespoon sesame oil

½ cup fresh spinach, chopped

½ cup carrots, shredded

½ cup fresh mushrooms, chopped

1 small zucchini, chopped

¼ small onion, chopped

1 tablespoon soy sauce

¼ teaspoon dry mustard

¼ teaspoon freshly ground pepper

¼ teaspoon garlic powder

1 package wonton skins

Soup:

4 cups chicken stock

2 cups beef stock

1 tablespoon soy sauce

3 green onions, chopped

1 cup fresh spinach

1. Pour oil into wok and set to SEAR.
2. Add spinach, carrots, mushrooms, zucchini and onions to wok; cook for 3 minutes.
3. Add soy sauce, mustard, pepper and garlic to wok; mix well.
4. Remove vegetable mixture from wok and let cool.
5. Add chicken and beef stock to wok and let simmer.
6. Place each wonton skin on a flat surface with one corner towards you like a diamond.
7. Place 1 teaspoon of vegetable mixture in the center of each wonton.
8. Moisten the wonton edges with water and fold one corner over to form a triangle; press to seal.
9. Bring the two points to the center of the wonton and press down with moist fingers.
10. Gently add all wontons to wok, 1 at a time; cook for 3 minutes.
11. Add soy sauce, green onions and spinach; cook for 1 minute and serve.

Tortilla Soup

Ingredients:

1 cup chicken, cooked and diced

4 cups chicken stock

1 can (10½ ounces) Mexican tomatoes with green chiles

1 tablespoon fresh cilantro leaves

½ teaspoon cumin

1 cup red kidney beans, cooked

1 cup corn

1 cup corn chips

½ cup Monterey Jack cheese, shredded

Green onions, chopped

1. Set wok to SEAR.
2. Add chicken, stock and tomatoes to wok; cover and cook for 10 minutes.
3. Add cilantro, cumin, kidney beans and corn to wok; cook for 5 minutes.
4. Ladle soup into bowls and top with corn chips, cheese and green onions.

Italian Wedding Soup

Meatballs:

½ cup onions, minced

¼ cup pesto sauce

1 large egg, beaten

1 teaspoon salt

½ teaspoon freshly ground pepper

½ teaspoon garlic powder

¼ cup Italian breadcrumbs

1 pound ground turkey breast

Soup:

8 cups chicken stock

1 pound Swiss chard, finely chopped and stems removed

2 large eggs, beaten

2 tablespoons Parmesan cheese, grated

1. Combine all meatball ingredients; mix well.
2. Shape mixture into 1-inch balls.
3. Add stock and Swiss chard to wok and set to SEAR; bring to a boil.
4. Add meatballs to wok; cover and cook for 15 minutes.
5. In a bowl, combine eggs and cheese; mix well.
6. While stirring with a wooden spoon, slowly pour egg mixture into broth.
7. Serve immediately.

Corn Chowder

Makes 6 to 8 servings

Ingredients:

2 tablespoons salted butter

½ cup onions, diced

¼ cup celery, diced

¼ cup carrots, diced

¼ cup ham, diced

1 red bell pepper, diced

2 russet potatoes, peeled and diced

1 teaspoon salt

½ teaspoon freshly ground pepper

4 ears of corn

4 cups chicken stock

2 cups heavy cream

Sour cream

Fresh cilantro, chopped

1. Set wok to MEDIUM.
2. Add butter to wok and let melt.
3. Add onions, celery and carrots to wok; cook for 3 minutes.
4. Add ham, peppers, potatoes, salt and pepper to wok; cover and cook for 5 minutes.
5. Cut the corn off the cobs, reserving the cobs.
6. Add corn, cobs and stock to wok; cover and cook for 20 minutes.
7. Remove cobs from wok and add cream; stir and cook for 5 minutes.
8. Ladle soup into bowls with a dab of sour cream and fresh cilantro.

Deb's Tip:
If you prefer a smoother consistency, use a blender to puree the soup.

Crab Asparagus Soup

Ingredients:

2 tablespoons salted butter

1 whole shallot, minced

1 garlic clove, minced

1 celery stalk, minced

6 cups chicken stock

1 teaspoon salt

¼ teaspoon white pepper

1 cup fresh or frozen asparagus, cut into 1-inch pieces

4 ounces cream cheese

1 cup heavy cream

2 tablespoons sherry

6 ounces lump blue crab

1. Set wok to MEDIUM.
2. Add butter to wok and let melt.
3. Add shallots to wok; cook for 1 minute.
4. Add garlic to wok; cook for 1 minute.
5. Add celery, chicken stock, salt and pepper to wok.
6. Increase wok to SEAR and let simmer for 15 minutes.
7. Add asparagus and cream cheese to wok; let simmer for 5 minutes.
8. Use a blender to puree soup to desired consistency.
9. Pour soup back into the wok.
10. Add cream, sherry and crab to wok; cook for 3 minutes and serve.

Minestrone Soup

Ingredients:

1 package (1 pound) mostaccioli pasta, cooked

6 cups beef stock

1 can (6 ounces) tomato paste

1 can (15 ounces) red kidney beans, rinsed and drained

1 can (15 ounces) chickpeas, rinsed and drained

1 can (14½ ounces) stewed tomatoes, with juice

1½ cups vegetable juice

2 teaspoons sugar

1 tablespoon fresh thyme

1 tablespoon fresh oregano

1 package (12 ounces) frozen mixed Italian vegetables

1 cup fresh spinach leaves, cut into strips

5 basil leaves, cut into strips

1. Set wok to SEAR.
2. Add stock and tomato paste to wok; stir well.
3. Add beans, chickpeas, tomatoes, vegetable juice and sugar to wok; stir.
4. Add thyme and oregano to wok; bring soup to a boil.
5. Add mixed vegetables to wok; stir and cover.
6. Reduce heat to MEDIUM and let simmer for 10 minutes.
7. Add pasta, spinach and basil to wok; cook for an additional 2 minutes.
8. Serve immediately.

Deb's Tip:
Top the soup with Parmesan cheese and serve with a piece of warm Italian bread.

Carrot Coriander Soup

Ingredients:

2 tablespoons unsalted butter

1 medium onion, finely chopped

1 teaspoon ground coriander

1 teaspoon salt

½ teaspoon freshly ground pepper

2 pounds carrots, peeled and thinly sliced

4 cups chicken stock

2 tablespoons orange juice

1. Set wok to MEDIUM.
2. Add butter, onions, coriander, salt and pepper to wok; cook for 3 minutes.
3. Increase wok to SEAR.
4. Add remaining ingredients to wok; cover and cook for 20 minutes.
5. Transfer soup to a blender and puree until desired consistency.

Deb's Tip:
Garnish with freshly chopped cilantro.

Easy Thai Pumpkin Soup

Makes 4 to 6 servings

Ingredients:

2 tablespoons sesame oil

2 tablespoons freshly grated ginger

1 tablespoon brown sugar

1 tablespoon Thai red curry paste

1 can (14 ounces) pumpkin puree

1 cup chicken stock

1 can (13½ ounces) coconut milk

1 tablespoon fish sauce

1. Pour oil into wok and set to SEAR.
2. Add ginger, sugar and curry paste to wok; cook for 1 minute.
3. Add remaining ingredients to wok; stir and cook for 10 minutes.
4. Serve immediately.

Deb's Tip:
Make this even better by using freshly roasted pumpkin or squash instead of the puree.

New England Seafood Chowder

Ingredients:

¼ cup salted butter

1 small onion, minced

1 celery stalk, finely chopped

¼ cup all-purpose flour

2 cups fish or chicken stock

½ pound red bliss potatoes, diced

1 teaspoon salt

½ teaspoon freshly ground pepper

1 pound cod, cut into 1-inch pieces

1 pound sea scallops

1 pound large shrimp, peeled and deveined

½ pound lobster meat

2 cups heavy cream

1 cup milk

2 tablespoons fresh parsley, chopped

1. Set wok to MEDIUM.
2. Add butter to wok and let melt.
3. Add onions and celery to wok; cook for 3 minutes.
4. Add flour to wok; stir to make a paste.
5. Add stock, potatoes, salt and pepper to wok; stir and cook for 10 minutes.
6. Add cod, scallops and shrimp to wok; cook for 3 minutes.
7. Add lobster, cream and milk to wok; cover and simmer for 3 minutes.
8. Garnish with parsley and serve.

Chicken & Dumpling Soup

Makes 6 servings

Ingredients:

2 cups chicken, cooked

8 cups chicken stock

1 cup frozen mixed vegetables

1 sprig of fresh thyme

Dumplings:

1 cup biscuit baking mix

¼ cup milk

1 tablespoon fresh parsley, chopped

1 teaspoon fresh rosemary leaves, chopped

1. Add stock, chicken, vegetables and thyme to wok.
2. Set wok to SEAR, cover and cook for 15 minutes.
3. In a bowl, combine dumpling ingredients; do not over-mix.
4. Using a teaspoon, drop batter into boiling soup; cover and cook for 10 minutes.
5. Ladle soup into bowls and serve.

Sautées & Stir-Frys

Sesame Orange Chicken

Makes 4 servings

Ingredients:

8 ounces boneless, skinless chicken breast, cubed

¼ cup cornstarch

1 large egg, beaten

1 cup flour

1 teaspoon salt

2 tablespoons sesame seeds

½ cup canola oil

Stir-Fry:

2 garlic cloves, minced

1 tablespoon ginger, chopped

1 red bell pepper, julienned

½ cup matchstick carrots

1 cup broccoli flowerets

2 tablespoons orange marmalade

¼ cup bottled stir-fry sauce

3 green onions, chopped

Orange zest

1. Place cornstarch in a zipper bag.
2. Pour egg into a bowl.
3. Combine flour, salt and sesame seeds on a plate.
4. Add chicken to zipper bag; shake well.
5. Dip chicken into egg and roll in flour mixture.
6. Pour oil into wok and set to SEAR.
7. Using a candy thermometer, measure oil temperature until it reaches 350 degrees.
8. Add 5 pieces of chicken to wok; cook for 3 minutes on each side.
9. Remove chicken and place on paper towels to drain excess oil.
10. Repeat with remaining chicken.
11. Add garlic and ginger to wok; cook for 1 minute.
12. Add peppers, carrots and broccoli to wok; cook for 2 minutes.
13. Add chicken, marmalade and stir-fry sauce to wok; toss well.
14. Sprinkle with green onions and orange zest.
15. Serve immediately.

Easy Mexican Stir-Fry

Ingredients:

2 tablespoons extra-virgin olive oil

1 pound boneless, skinless chicken breast, cut into thin strips

1 medium onion, cut into thin strips

1 bell pepper, cut into thin strips

1 envelope fajita seasoning mix

1 cup corn

1 cup red kidney beans, cooked

1 can (10½ ounces) Mexican tomatoes with cilantro and lime

1 cup chicken stock

2 cups corn chips

½ cup Mexican cheese, shredded

Sour cream

Green onions, chopped

1. Pour oil into wok and set to SEAR.
2. Add chicken to wok; cook for 3 minutes on each side.
3. Add onions, peppers and seasoning to wok; toss well and cook for 3 minutes.
4. Reduce wok to MEDIUM.
5. Add corn, beans, tomatoes and stock to wok; cover and cook for 15 minutes; toss well.
6. Top with corn chips and cheese; cover and cook for 5 minutes.
7. Garnish with sour cream and chopped green onions.
8. Serve immediately.

Deb's Tip:
Try skirt steak instead of chicken.

Beef Stir-Fry

Makes 6 servings

Marinade:

¼ cup soy sauce

¼ cup sesame oil

2 tablespoons dry white wine

1 teaspoon sugar

1 tablespoon cornstarch

1 cup chicken stock

Stir-Fry:

1½ pounds sirloin, cut into thin strips

1 medium onion, sliced

3 garlic cloves, minced

1 tablespoon ginger, grated

1 cup fresh or frozen stir-fry vegetables

1 can (8 ounces) water chestnuts, sliced

1 can (8 ounces) bamboo shoots

1. In a bowl, combine marinade ingredients.
2. Add meat to the bowl and let marinate for 20 minutes.
3. Remove meat, reserving the liquid.
4. Set wok to SEAR.
5. Add meat and onions to wok; cook for 3 minutes.
6. Add garlic and ginger to wok; cook for 2 minutes.
7. Add vegetables, water chestnuts, bamboo shoots and reserved marinade to wok; bring to a boil.
8. Serve immediately.

Stir-Fry Vegetables

Ingredients:

2 tablespoons sesame oil

2 garlic cloves

1 tablespoon freshly grated ginger

1 medium onion, thinly sliced

1 cup carrots, cut diagonally

2 cups broccoli flowerets

2 cups sugar snap peas

1 red bell pepper, julienned

¼ cup bottled stir-fry sauce

2 teaspoons toasted sesame seeds

1. Pour oil into wok and set to SEAR.
2. Add garlic and ginger to wok; cook for 1 minute.
3. Add all vegetables to wok; toss and cook for 3 minutes.
4. Add stir-fry sauce to wok; toss well.
5. Sprinkle with sesame seeds and serve.

Orange Sesame Pork

Marinade:

1 cup orange juice

½ cup soy sauce

1 tablespoon cornstarch

Stir-Fry:

1 pound pork tenderloin, cut into thin strips

2 tablespoons sesame oil

1 tablespoon ginger, minced

1 garlic clove, minced

6 cups stir-fry vegetables, fresh or frozen

1 tablespoon sugar

2 teaspoons sesame seeds

1. In a bowl, combine marinade ingredients; mix well.
2. Place pork into the bowl and let marinate for 30 minutes.
3. Pour oil into wok and set to SEAR.
4. Add ginger and garlic to wok; cook for 1 minute.
5. Add pork to wok, reserving the marinade; cook for 4 minutes.
6. Add vegetables, sugar and reserved marinade to wok; bring to a boil.
7. Add sesame seeds to wok; toss well and serve.

Deb's Tip:
Add mandarin oranges to this dish for extra texture and flavor.

Balsamic Pork Stir-Fry

Ingredients:

2 tablespoons extra-virgin olive oil

1 pound pork loin, cut into thin strips

1 medium onion, thinly sliced

½ cup carrots, sliced

½ teaspoon whole fennel seeds

1 tablespoon brown sugar

1 teaspoon salt

½ teaspoon freshly ground pepper

¼ cup dried cranberries

1 apple, cored and sliced

1 teaspoon cornstarch

¼ cup chicken stock

1 tablespoon balsamic vinegar

1. Pour oil into wok and set to SEAR.
2. Add pork to wok; cook for 2 minutes on each side.
3. Add onions and carrots to wok; cook for 4 minutes.
4. Add fennel, sugar, salt and pepper to wok; toss.
5. Add cranberries and apples to wok; toss well.
6. In a bowl, dissolve the cornstarch in chicken stock.
7. Add stock and vinegar to wok; cook for 3 minutes or until boiling.
8. Serve immediately.

Deb's Tip:
Try raisins instead of cranberries and serve over buttered noodles.

Chicken Red Thai Curry

Ingredients:

1 tablespoon sesame oil

8 ounces boneless, skinless chicken breast, diced into 1-inch cubes

1 medium onion, thinly sliced

1 red bell pepper, julienned

3 garlic cloves, minced

1 tablespoon fresh ginger, minced

1 tablespoon red curry paste

1 can (13½ ounces) coconut milk

1 teaspoon soy sauce

1 teaspoon rice wine vinegar

1 tablespoon brown sugar

1 can (8 ounces) bamboo shoots, drained

1. Pour oil into wok and set to SEAR.
2. Add chicken to wok; cook for 3 minutes on each side.
3. Add onions and peppers to wok; cook for 2 minutes.
4. Add garlic, ginger and curry paste to wok; stir and cook for 1 minute.
5. Add coconut milk, soy sauce, vinegar and sugar to wok; reduce liquid for 15 minutes.
6. Add bamboo shoots to wok; toss well.
7. Serve immediately.

Deb's Tip:
This dish is amazing served over thinly sliced zucchini or yellow squash.

Sea Scallops Cantonese

Ingredients:

1 pound jumbo sea scallops

2 tablespoons sesame oil

1 tablespoon ginger, minced

2 garlic cloves, minced

1 red bell pepper, julienned

1 cup fresh stir-fry vegetables, cut uniform

¼ cup bottled stir-fry sauce

1 tablespoon rice wine vinegar

4 green onions, chopped

1. Wash and pat dry scallops with paper towels.
2. Pour oil into wok and set to SEAR.
3. Add ginger and garlic to wok; cook for 1 minute.
4. Add sea scallops to wok; cook for 2 minutes on each side.
5. Add peppers to wok; cook for 2 minutes.
6. Add remaining ingredients to wok; toss and cook for 3 minutes.
7. Serve immediately.

Shrimp Pad Thai

Ingredients:

8 ounces Thai rice noodles, soaked

2 tablespoons sesame oil

1 tablespoon freshly grated ginger

2 garlic cloves

8 jumbo shrimp, peeled and deveined

1 large egg, beaten

1 package (3¼ ounces) Pad Thai sauce

½ cup dry roasted peanuts, chopped

3 green onions, chopped

3 cups fresh bean sprouts

1 tablespoon fresh lime juice

¼ cup fresh cilantro, chopped

1. Pour oil into wok and set to SEAR.
2. Add ginger and garlic to wok; cook for 1 minute.
3. Add shrimp to wok; cook for 3 minutes on each side.
4. Transfer shrimp to a plate.
5. Pour egg into wok; scramble for 30 seconds.
6. Drain rice noodles and add to wok; cook for 4 minutes.
7. Add Pad Thai sauce, peanuts, green onions and bean sprouts to wok; toss and cook for 4 minutes.
8. Top with lime juice and cilantro.
9. Serve immediately.

Stir-Fry Chicken & Cashews

Ingredients:

2 tablespoons sesame oil

½ pound boneless, skinless chicken breast, cut into strips

1 small onion, thinly sliced

½ cup baby corn, cut in half lengthwise

1 red bell pepper, julienned

½ cup cashews

2 teaspoons sugar

¼ cup bottled stir-fry sauce

3 green onions, chopped

1. Pour oil into wok and set to SEAR.
2. Add chicken and onions to wok; cook for 3 minutes on each side.
3. Add corn, peppers, cashews and sugar to wok; cook for 3 minutes.
4. Add stir-fry sauce to wok; stir and cook for 3 minutes.
5. Sprinkle with green onions and serve.

Chicken Chow Mein

Makes 6 servings

Ingredients:

10 ounces lo mein noodles, cooked

1 pound boneless, skinless chicken breast, cubed

2 tablespoons sesame oil

1 tablespoon freshly grated ginger

2 garlic cloves, minced

1 carrot, peeled and thinly sliced

1 cup snow peas

3 cabbage leaves, sliced

1 cup bean sprouts

3 green onions, chopped

Marinade:

3 tablespoons rice wine vinegar

3 tablespoons soy sauce

2 teaspoons cornstarch

½ cup chicken stock

1. In a bowl, combine marinade ingredients.
2. Add chicken to bowl and let marinate for 20 minutes.
3. Pour oil into wok and set to SEAR.
4. Add chicken to wok, reserving the marinade; cook for 3 minutes on each side.
5. Add ginger and garlic to wok; cook for 2 minutes.
6. Add carrots, snow peas, cabbage and bean sprouts to wok; toss and cook for 3 minutes.
7. Add noodles, chicken and reserved marinade to wok; toss and cook until bubbly.
8. Garnish with chopped green onions and serve.

Beef Medallions In Brandy Sauce

Makes 4 servings

Ingredients:

1 pound beef filet, cut into ¼-inch slices

1 teaspoon salt

½ teaspoon freshly ground pepper

2 tablespoons extra-virgin olive oil

1 large shallot, minced

8 ounces mushrooms, sliced

½ cup brandy

½ cup beef stock

½ cup heavy cream

1 tablespoon fresh parsley, chopped

1. Season steak with salt and pepper.
2. Pour oil into wok and set to SEAR.
3. Add 3 slices of steak to wok; cook for 3 minutes on each side.
4. Repeat with remaining steak; transfer cooked steak to a plate.
5. Add shallots to wok; cook for 1 minute.
6. Add mushrooms to wok; cook for 3 minutes.
7. Add brandy and stock to wok; let simmer for 5 minutes.
8. Add heavy cream to wok.
9. Place steak back into wok; stir and cook for 3 minutes.
10. Sprinkle with chopped parsley and serve.

Pepper Steak

Ingredients:

2 tablespoons extra-virgin olive oil

1 pound beef sirloin, cut into thin strips

1 medium onion, julienned

1 large red bell pepper, julienned

1 teaspoon salt

½ teaspoon freshly ground pepper

1 envelope brown gravy mix

1 cup water

1. Pour oil into wok and set to SEAR.
2. Add steak, onions, peppers, salt and pepper to wok; cook for 5 minutes.
3. In a bowl, dissolve gravy mix in water and pour into wok; bring to a boil.
4. Serve immediately.

Deb's Tip:
Add a pound of sliced button mushrooms for extra flavor.

Asparagus Stir-Fry

Ingredients:

2 tablespoons extra-virgin olive oil

1 pound asparagus, cut into 2-inch pieces

1 teaspoon cornstarch

¼ cup chicken stock

½ teaspoon ginger, grated

½ cup mushrooms, sliced

1 red bell pepper, julienned

2 teaspoons soy sauce

2 green onions, chopped

1 teaspoon sesame seeds

1. Pour oil into wok and set to SEAR.
2. Add asparagus to wok; cook for 2 minutes.
3. In a bowl, dissolve cornstarch in chicken stock.
4. Add ginger, mushrooms and peppers to wok; cook for 2 minutes.
5. Pour stock and soy sauce into wok; stir and cook until bubbly.
6. Sprinkle with green onions and sesame seeds.
7. Serve immediately.

Vegetable Lo Mein

Ingredients:

8 ounces lo mein noodles, cooked

2 tablespoons sesame oil

2 garlic cloves, minced

1 tablespoon freshly grated ginger

1 small onion, thinly sliced

1 red bell pepper, julienned

½ cup matchstick carrots

1 can (8 ounces) stir-fry vegetables, drained

2 tablespoons bottled stir-fry sauce

3 green onions, chopped

1. Pour oil into wok and set to SEAR.
2. Add garlic and ginger to wok; cook for 1 minute.
3. Add onions, peppers, carrots and stir-fry vegetables to wok; cook for 3 minutes.
4. Add noodles and stir-fry sauce to wok; stir.
5. Sprinkle with chopped green onions and serve.

Sweet & Sour Chicken

Makes 4 servings

Ingredients:

2 tablespoons soy sauce

2 tablespoons cornstarch

2 tablespoons sesame oil

1 pound boneless, skinless chicken breast, cut into 1-inch cubes

1 container (12 ounces) sweet and sour sauce

1 can (20 ounces) pineapple chunks, drained

1 can (28 ounces) Oriental mixed vegetables, drained

½ cup mandarin oranges, sliced and drained

12 maraschino cherries, halved

1. In a bowl, combine soy sauce and cornstarch; mix well.
2. Add chicken to bowl; let marinate for 30 minutes.
3. Pour oil into wok and set to SEAR.
4. Add chicken to wok; cook for 3 minutes on each side.
5. Add sweet and sour sauce to wok; stir.
6. Add remaining ingredients to wok; cook for 5 minutes until sauce thickens and comes to a boil.
7. Serve immediately.

Beef Teriyaki

Ingredients:

1 pound top sirloin, sliced into thin strips

½ cup teriyaki sauce

2 tablespoons sesame oil

1 medium onion, thinly sliced

1 red bell pepper, julienned

2 cups frozen green beans

1. In a bowl, marinate steak in teriyaki sauce for 20 minutes.
2. Pour oil into wok and set to SEAR.
3. Add steak to wok, reserving the marinade; cook steak for 3 minutes on each side.
4. Add onions and peppers to wok; cook for 3 minutes.
5. Add green beans and marinade to wok; cook for 5 minutes.
6. Serve immediately.

Pasta, Seafood & Some Ideas

Angel Hair Pasta With Chicken & Sausage

Makes 4 to 6 servings

Ingredients:

1 pound angel hair pasta, cooked al dente

2 tablespoons extra-virgin olive oil

½ pound boneless, skinless chicken breast, cut into 1-inch cubes

½ pound sweet Italian sausage, cooked and sliced

1 medium onion, thinly sliced

1 red bell pepper, cut into strips

1 teaspoon granulated garlic

1 teaspoon Italian seasoning

2 cups pasta sauce

3 tablespoons Parmesan cheese, grated

1. Pour oil into wok and set to SEAR.
2. Add chicken to wok; cook for 2 minutes on each side.
3. Add sausage and onions to wok; cook for 3 minutes.
4. Add peppers, garlic and Italian seasoning to wok; toss well.
5. Add pasta sauce to wok; cover and cook for 10 minutes.
6. Add angel hair pasta and cheese to wok; toss and serve.

Garden Scallop Pasta

Ingredients:

8 ounces linguini, cooked al dente

1 pound sea scallops

2 tablespoons extra-virgin olive oil

1 shallot, minced

2 garlic cloves, minced

1 teaspoon salt

½ teaspoon freshly ground pepper

1 cup broccoli flowerets

1 cup spinach leaves

1 cup chicken stock

4 ounces cream cheese

½ cup Romano cheese, grated

1. Wash and pat dry scallops with paper towels.
2. Pour oil into wok and set to SEAR.
3. Add shallots and garlic to wok; cook for 1 minute.
4. Add scallops, salt and pepper to wok; cook for 3 minutes on each side.
5. Add broccoli and spinach to wok; toss well.
6. Add stock to wok; bring to a simmer.
7. Add cream cheese to wok; stir until dissolved.
8. Add linguini to wok; toss well.
9. Turn off wok, top with Romano cheese and serve.

Deb's Tip:
A terrific addition to this dish is a quarter cup of sliced mushrooms.

Ratatouille Fusilli

Ingredients:

1 pound fusilli pasta, cooked al dente

2 tablespoons extra-virgin olive oil

1 medium onion, thinly sliced

2 garlic cloves, minced

1 medium eggplant, peeled and cut into 1-inch cubes

1 zucchini, cut into ¼-inch rounds

1 teaspoon salt

½ teaspoon freshly ground pepper

1 can (14½ ounces) tomatoes with basil

2 tablespoons Parmesan cheese, grated

1. Pour oil into wok and set to SEAR.
2. Add onions to wok; cook for 2 minutes.
3. Add garlic to wok; cook for 1 minute.
4. Add eggplant, zucchini, salt and pepper to wok; cook for 3 minutes.
5. Add tomatoes to wok; cover and cook for 5 minutes.
6. Add pasta and cheese to wok; toss well.
7. Serve immediately.

Spinach Fettuccine With Bleu Cheese Alfredo

Makes 6 to 8 servings

Ingredients:

1 pound spinach fettuccine, cooked al dente

2 garlic cloves, minced

3 tablespoons salted butter

1 cup heavy cream

1 teaspoon salt

½ teaspoon freshly cracked pepper

½ cup Parmesan cheese, grated

½ cup bleu cheese, crumbled

2 tablespoons fresh Italian parsley, chopped

1. Set wok to MEDIUM.
2. Add garlic and butter to wok; cook for 2 minutes.
3. Increase wok to HIGH.
4. Add cream to wok; let simmer for 2 minutes.
5. Add fettuccine, salt and pepper to wok; toss and cook for 1 minute.
6. Turn off wok.
7. Add cheeses to wok; toss well.
8. Garnish with parsley and serve.

Pasta Primavera

Ingredients:

8 ounces linguini, cooked al dente

½ cup chicken stock

¼ cup white wine

1 package (8 ounces) cream cheese, cut into 4 pieces

1 cup broccoli flowerets

1 carrot, thinly sliced

1 red bell pepper, julienned

1 yellow squash, thinly sliced

½ cup Parmesan cheese, grated

1 teaspoon salt

½ teaspoon freshly ground pepper

1 tablespoon fresh parsley, chopped

1. Set wok to SEAR.
2. Add stock and wine to wok; bring to a boil.
3. Whisk 1 piece of cream cheese at a time into boiling liquid until smooth.
4. Add vegetables to wok; cook for 3 minutes.
5. Add pasta, cheese, salt and pepper to wok; toss.
6. Garnish with parsley and serve.

Vegetable Fried Brown Rice

Makes 4 to 6 servings

Ingredients:

4 cups brown rice, cooked

2 tablespoons sesame oil

1 garlic clove, minced

2 cups matchstick carrots

1 red bell pepper, julienned

1 large zucchini, thinly sliced

1 yellow squash, thinly sliced

8 ounces mushrooms, sliced

2 cups bean sprouts

2 tablespoons soy sauce

2 tablespoons bottled stir-fry sauce

4 green onions, chopped

1. Pour oil into wok and set to SEAR.
2. Add garlic and carrots to wok; cook for 1 minute.
3. Add remaining vegetables, except onions, to wok; cook for 2 minutes.
4. Add rice to wok; cook for 3 minutes.
5. Add soy and stir-fry sauce to wok; toss.
6. Sprinkle with green onions and serve.

Zucchini & Tomatoes

Makes 2 to 4 servings

Ingredients:

2 tablespoons extra-virgin olive oil

1 small onion, minced

2 garlic cloves, minced

2 zucchini, cut into thin strips

1 can (14½ ounces) petite diced tomatoes

1 teaspoon salt

½ teaspoon freshly ground pepper

½ teaspoon oregano

3 tablespoons Parmesan cheese, grated

1. Pour oil into wok and set to SEAR.
2. Add onions and garlic to wok; cook for 2 minutes.
3. Add zucchini to wok; cook for 2 minutes.
4. Add tomatoes and seasonings to wok; toss and cook for 3 minutes.
5. Add cheese to wok; stir well.
6. Serve immediately.

Angel Hair Pasta With Tomatoes

Ingredients:

½ pound angel hair pasta, cooked al dente

¼ cup extra-virgin olive oil

1 small onion, minced

3 garlic cloves, minced

2 tablespoons tomato paste

1 teaspoon salt

½ teaspoon freshly ground pepper

1 cup fresh tomatoes, diced

1 cup chicken stock

1 tablespoon fresh parsley, chopped

6 basil leaves, torn

Parmesan cheese, grated

1. Pour oil into wok and set to SEAR.
2. Add onions, garlic, paste, salt and pepper to wok; cook for 3 minutes.
3. Add tomatoes and chicken stock to wok; cook for 5 minutes.
4. Add parsley, basil and angel hair pasta to wok; toss well.
5. Top with Parmesan cheese and serve.

Meaty Mushroom Rigatoni

Ingredients:

1 pound rigatoni, cooked al dente

1 pound ground beef

½ cup onions, diced

2 garlic cloves, minced

1 cup mushrooms, sliced

½ teaspoon garlic powder

1 teaspoon salt

½ teaspoon freshly ground pepper

2 tablespoons tomato paste

½ cup beef stock

1 can (28 ounces) petite diced tomatoes

1 sprig of fresh thyme

¾ cup Mozzarella cheese, shredded

¼ cup Parmesan cheese, grated

1. Place beef into wok and set to SEAR.
2. Break up beef with a wooden spoon while cooking for 4 minutes; drain fat and place beef back into the wok.
3. Add onions, garlic, mushrooms, garlic powder, salt and pepper to wok; stir and cook for 3 minutes.
4. Add tomato paste to wok; stir and cook for 3 minutes.
5. Add beef stock, tomatoes and thyme to wok; cover and reduce heat to MEDIUM; cook for 25 minutes.
6. Remove thyme and add rigatoni to wok; mix well.
7. Add cheeses to wok; cover and cook for 3 minutes.
8. Serve immediately.

Chicken Cacciatore

Ingredients:

2 tablespoons extra-virgin olive oil

1 pound boneless, skinless chicken breast, cut into strips

1 medium onion, thinly sliced

1 green bell pepper, julienned

8 ounces mushrooms, sliced

½ teaspoon Italian seasoning

1 teaspoon salt

½ teaspoon freshly ground pepper

½ cup black olives, pitted

1 jar (26 ounces) pasta sauce

1. Pour oil into wok and set to SEAR.
2. Add chicken to wok; cook for 3 minutes.
3. Add onions and peppers to wok; cook for 3 minutes.
4. Add mushrooms, Italian seasoning, salt and pepper to wok; stir.
5. Add olives and pasta sauce to wok; bring to a simmer.
6. Serve immediately.

Deb's Tip:
Serve with your favorite rice or pasta.

Bucatini Carbonara

Ingredients:

8 ounces bucatini, cooked al dente

8 ounces bacon, cut into 1-inch pieces

1 medium onion, finely chopped

¼ cup chicken stock

3 large eggs, beaten

¼ cup heavy cream

½ cup Parmesan cheese, grated

1 teaspoon salt

½ teaspoon freshly ground pepper

3 green onions, chopped

1. Place bacon into wok and set to SEAR; cook for 3 minutes.
2. Remove bacon and place on paper towels to drain excess fat.
3. Drain fat from wok.
4. Add onions to wok; cook for 3 minutes.
5. Add chicken stock to wok.
6. In a bowl, combine eggs, heavy cream, cheese, salt and pepper.
7. Add bucatini and egg mixture to wok; let heat until bubbly.
8. Reduce wok to KEEP WARM.
9. Add bacon and green onions to wok; toss and serve.

Linguini With White Clam Sauce

Ingredients:

1 pound linguini, cooked al dente

2 cans (6½ ounces each) chopped clams in juice

3 tablespoons extra-virgin olive oil

1 small onion, finely chopped

3 garlic cloves, minced

1 cup dry white wine

1 cup chicken stock

2 tablespoons salted butter, cut into small pieces

1 teaspoon salt

½ teaspoon freshly ground pepper

2 tablespoons fresh pesto

2 tablespoons fresh parsley, chopped

1. Drain clams reserving the liquid.

2. Pour oil into wok and set to SEAR.

3. Add onions and garlic to wok; cook for 1 minute.

4. Add wine, stock and reserved clam juice to wok; cook for 10 minutes.

5. Add butter to wok, 1 piece at a time; whisk until dissolved.

6. Add clams, linguini, salt and pepper to wok; toss and cook for 3 minutes.

7. Add pesto and parsley to wok; toss well and serve.

Vegetarian Pasta

Ingredients:

8 ounces pappardelle pasta, cooked

2 tablespoons extra-virgin olive oil

1 onion, thinly sliced

2 garlic cloves, minced

1 teaspoon salt

½ teaspoon freshly ground pepper

2 cups tomatoes, diced and seeds removed

½ cup northern white beans, cooked

2 roasted red peppers, julienned

½ cup chicken stock

1 cup fresh Swiss chard

½ cup Parmesan cheese, grated

1. Pour oil into wok and set to SEAR.
2. Add onions to wok; cook for 1 minute.
3. Add garlic, salt and pepper to wok; cook for 1 minute.
4. Add tomatoes, beans and peppers to wok; cook for 5 minutes.
5. Add stock, pasta and Swiss chard to wok; stir and cook for 2 minutes.
6. Turn off wok and sprinkle with Parmesan cheese.
7. Serve immediately.

Shrimp Pasta With Feta Cheese

Makes 4 servings

Ingredients:

½ pound penne pasta, cooked

2 tablespoons extra-virgin olive oil

1 pound large shrimp, peeled and deveined

1 teaspoon dry oregano

1 teaspoon salt

½ teaspoon freshly ground pepper

3 garlic cloves, minced

1 teaspoon lemon juice

1 can (28 ounces) petite diced tomatoes

½ cup black olives, pitted

½ cup feta cheese, crumbled

Fresh parsley, chopped

1. Pour oil into wok and set to SEAR.
2. Add shrimp, oregano, salt and pepper to wok; stir and cook for 3 minutes on each side.
3. Add garlic and lemon juice to wok; stir.
4. Add tomatoes to wok; cover and cook for 5 minutes.
5. Add penne and olives to wok; toss well.
6. Add feta cheese to wok; cover until cheese begins to melt.
7. Garnish with parsley and serve.

th Watering Mussels

Ingredients:

2 pounds mussels, scrubbed and beards removed

2 tablespoons extra-virgin olive oil

3 garlic cloves, minced

1 shallot, minced

½ cup dry white wine

½ cup chicken stock

1 teaspoon salt

½ teaspoon freshly ground pepper

1 tablespoon fresh parsley, chopped

1. Pour oil into wok and set to SEAR.
2. Add garlic and shallots to wok; cook for 1 minute.
3. Add wine, stock, salt and pepper to wok; cook for 4 minutes.
4. Add mussels to wok; toss and cover.
5. Let cook for 5 minutes or until mussels open completely.
6. Add parsley to wok; toss and serve.

Deb's Tip:
Serve in deep bowls with the broth and a crusty bread.

Gluten Free Buffalo Chicken

Ingredients:

8 ounces boneless, skinless chicken breast, cut into 1-inch cubes

1 large egg, beaten

1 cup Parmesan cheese, grated

2 tablespoons salted butter

¼ cup Louisiana hot sauce

1 teaspoon white wine vinegar

1 teaspoon soy sauce

1 teaspoon ketchup

1. Pour egg into a bowl.
2. Spread cheese on a plate.
3. Dip chicken in egg and roll in cheese.
4. Set wok to SEAR.
5. Add 5 pieces of chicken to wok; cook for 3 minutes on each side.
6. Transfer chicken to a plate.
7. Repeat with remaining chicken.
8. Reduce wok to MEDIUM.
9. Add remaining ingredients to wok; cook until butter is melted.
10. Turn off wok; add chicken to wok and toss well.
11. Serve immediately.

Deb's Tip:
Serve over a tossed salad with cherry tomatoes and bleu cheese dressing.

Seafood Pasta Arrabbiata

Ingredients:

2 cups fusilli, cooked

½ pound jumbo shrimp, peeled and deveined

½ pound sea scallops

3 tablespoons extra-virgin olive oil

1 teaspoon salt

½ teaspoon freshly ground pepper

12 mussels, beards removed and scrubbed

4 garlic cloves, minced

1 shallot, minced

1 can (28 ounces) petite diced tomatoes

½ teaspoon crushed red pepper flakes

6 fresh basil leaves, torn

1 tablespoon fresh parsley, chopped

1. Wash and pat dry shrimp and scallops with paper towels.
2. Pour oil into wok and set to SEAR.
3. Add shrimp, scallops, salt and pepper to wok; cook for 2 minutes on each side.
4. Add mussels to wok; cook for 3 minutes.
5. Add garlic and shallots to wok; toss and cook until mussels start opening.
6. Add tomatoes and red pepper flakes to wok; cover and cook for 5 minutes.
7. Add fusilli to wok; toss and cook for 3 minutes.
8. Add basil to wok; toss.
9. Garnish with parsley and serve.

Shrimp Green Curry

Ingredients:

2 tablespoons sesame oil

1 tablespoon freshly grated ginger

1½ pounds large shrimp, peeled and deveined

1 teaspoon sugar

2 tablespoons green curry paste

2 tablespoons fish sauce

1 can (13½ ounces) coconut milk

4 basil leaves, shredded

1. Pour oil into wok and set to SEAR.
2. Add ginger and shrimp to wok; cook for 3 minutes on each side.
3. Transfer shrimp to a plate.
4. Add sugar, curry paste, fish sauce and coconut milk to wok; stir and cook for 8 minutes or until mixture thickens.
5. Add shrimp to wok; toss and cook for 1 minute.
6. Garnish with basil and serve.

Steamed Blue Crabs

Ingredients:
2 cups water

1 cup cider vinegar

1 lemon, sliced

12 large live blue crabs

Seasoning Mix:
¼ cup sea salt

3 tablespoons seafood seasoning salt

2 tablespoons celery seed

1. Set wok to SEAR.
2. Add water, vinegar and lemon to wok; bring to a boil.
3. In a bowl, combine seasoning mix ingredients.
4. Add 6 crabs to wok; sprinkle with half the seasoning mix; cover.
5. Cook for 15 minutes and remove crabs to a platter.
6. Repeat with remaining crabs and serve.

Deb's Tip:
Serve with melted butter and lemons.

Sausage & Peppers

Makes 4 to 6 servings

Ingredients:

1½ pounds Italian sausage

2 tablespoons extra-virgin olive oil

2 tablespoons balsamic vinegar

1 large onion, thinly sliced

1 teaspoon salt

½ teaspoon freshly ground pepper

1 teaspoon Italian seasoning

1 red bell pepper, julienned

1 green bell pepper, julienned

1 large zucchini, sliced

1. Pour oil into wok and set to SEAR.
2. Add sausage to wok; cook 4 minutes on each side.
3. Remove sausage and drain fat.
4. Slice sausage into 1-inch pieces.
5. Add sausage and remaining ingredients to wok; cook for 4 minutes.
6. Serve immediately.

Deb's Tip:
Serve on a crusty roll with melted cheese.

Sweet Treats

Caramel Popcorn Balls

Makes 6 servings

Ingredients:

6 cups popcorn, freshly popped
Butter-flavored non-stick cooking spray
¼ cup unsalted butter
1 cup sugar
1 cup dark corn syrup
½ teaspoon salt

1. Spray a 9 X 13 baking pan with non-stick spray.
2. Spread popcorn on baking pan.
3. Add butter, sugar and corn syrup to wok; stir.
4. Turn wok to SEAR.
5. Using a candy thermometer, measure temperature until it reaches 230 degrees; do not stir.
6. Pour mixture over popcorn; toss gently.
7. Let cool and shape popcorn into balls.

Deb's Tip:
To make a perfect gift, wrap popcorn balls in cellophane and tie them with a bow.

Lollipops

Ingredients:

Parchment paper

Non-stick cooking spray

1 cup sugar

½ cup light corn syrup

½ cup water

¼ teaspoon cream of tartar

4 drops food coloring

1 teaspoon vanilla

6 lollipop sticks

1. Line cookie sheet with parchment paper.
2. Apply non-stick spray to parchment paper.
3. Add sugar, corn syrup, water and cream of tartar to wok; stir until sugar is dissolved.
4. Set wok to SEAR; do not stir.
5. Using a candy thermometer, measure temperature until it reaches 300 degrees; turn off wok.
6. Allow candy to cool to 270 degrees.
7. Add food coloring and vanilla to wok; stir.
8. Pour half the mixture immediately into a glass measuring cup.
9. Pour 2-inch circles onto the parchment paper, leaving 4 inches of space between the circles.
10. Place 1 lollipop stick into each circle so that the tip of the stick is in the center of the circle.
11. Pour the remaining syrup over each circle, securing the sticks in place.
12. Let cool completely before removing lollipops from parchment paper.
13. Wrap lollipops in small plastic lollipop bags or wax paper; store at room temperature.

Crystal Candy Ornaments

Ingredients:

Parchment paper

Butter-flavored non-stick cooking spray

10 small cookie cutters

1½ cups sugar

½ cup water

¼ cup light corn syrup

½ tablespoon cream of tartar

⅛ teaspoon gel food coloring

1. Line a jelly roll pan with parchment paper.
2. Apply non-stick spray to parchment paper.
3. Lightly spray the inside of the cookie cutters with non-stick spray and place on parchment paper.
4. Add sugar, water, corn syrup and cream of tartar to wok; stir.
5. Set wok to SEAR and bring mixture to a boil.
6. Using a candy thermometer, measure temperature until it reaches 300 degrees; turn off wok.
7. Add food coloring to wok; stir.
8. Pour mixture immediately into a glass measuring cup.
9. Pour mixture into each cookie cutter mold to cover the bottom, about ¼-inch thick.
10. Let cool completely before removing the molds.

Candy Cinnamon Pecans

Ingredients:

Parchment paper

Butter-flavored non-stick cooking spray

1 cup granulated sugar

½ teaspoon Chinese five-spice powder

⅛ teaspoon cream of tartar

¼ cup water

½ teaspoon vanilla

1½ cups pecans

1. Line a jelly roll pan with parchment paper.
2. Apply non-stick spray to parchment paper.
3. Add sugar, five-spice, cream of tartar and water to wok; mix well.
4. Set wok to SEAR.
5. Using a candy thermometer, measure temperature until it reaches 246 degrees.
6. Turn off wok.
7. Add vanilla and pecans to wok; stir until pecans are covered.
8. Pour nut mixture into prepared pan.
9. Place pan in oven at 350 degrees for 20 minutes.
10. Remove from oven, let cool and serve.

Marshmallow Cereal Treats

Ingredients:

Parchment paper

Butter-flavored non-stick cooking spray

3 tablespoons unsalted butter

1 bag (10 ounces) mini marshmallows

3 cups toasted oat cereal

3 cups fruit flavored cereal

1. Line a 9 X 9 inch baking pan with parchment paper.
2. Apply non-stick spray to pan.
3. Add butter and marshmallows to wok.
4. Set wok to HIGH and stir until melted.
5. Add cereals to wok; mix well.
6. Pour cereal mixture into prepared pan.
7. Place a sheet of parchment paper onto the pan and press down until firm.
8. Let cool for 30 minutes.
9. Cut into squares and serve.

Deb's Tip:
Instead of fruit cereal, try peanut butter or chocolate flavored cereal.

Fall Festival Caramel Apples

Ingredients:

10 large apples	2 cups corn syrup
10 craft sticks	½ cup unsalted butter
Parchment paper	2 cups heavy cream
1 cup granulated sugar	1 teaspoon vanilla
1 cup light brown sugar	

1. Wash and dry apples.
2. Insert a stick into the stem end of each apple.
3. Place apples on a baking sheet lined with parchment paper.
4. Add sugars, syrup, butter and cream to wok; whisk until smooth.
5. Turn wok to SEAR.
6. Using a candy thermometer, measure temperature until it reaches 248 degrees; turn off wok.
7. Add vanilla to wok; stir.
8. Let caramel rest for 5 minutes.
9. Dip apples into caramel and place them onto the baking sheet.
10. Let cool for 1 hour before serving.

Deb's Tip:
Drizzle white chocolate over apples and decorate with assorted candies.

Cherries Jubilee

Ingredients:

4 cups frozen cherries, thawed
½ cup sugar
2 tablespoons cornstarch
½ cup brandy
Vanilla ice cream

1. Strain cherries, reserving the juice.
2. In a bowl, combine reserved juice, sugar and cornstarch; mix well.
3. Pour mixture into wok and set to SEAR; cook until thickened.
4. Add cherries to wok; stir and cook for 3 minutes.
5. Add brandy to wok.
6. Serve with vanilla ice cream.

Deb's Tip:
Try kirsch instead of brandy.

Peppermint Divinity

Ingredients:

Butter-flavored non-stick cooking spray

Parchment paper

2 large egg whites, room temperature

¼ teaspoon salt

2½ cups sugar

½ cup water

½ cup light corn syrup

½ teaspoon peppermint extract

¼ cup peppermint candy, chopped

1. Line a cookie sheet with parchment paper.
2. Apply non-stick spray to parchment paper.
3. Using a mixer on high, beat egg whites and salt until stiff peaks forms.
4. In a bowl, combine sugar, water and corn syrup; mix well.
5. Pour syrup mixture into wok and set to SEAR.
6. Using a candy thermometer, measure temperature until it reaches 260 degrees; do not stir.
7. Turn off wok.
8. Pour candy mixture immediately into a glass measuring cup.
9. Using a mixer on high, slowly pour syrup into the egg whites in a thin and steady stream; beat mixture for 10 minutes.
10. Add extract to mixer and beat on high for 1 additional minute.
11. Drop heaping tablespoons of mixture onto cookie sheet, ½-inch apart.
12. Sprinkle with peppermint candy; let cool.
13. Store in an airtight container at room temperature for up to 7 days.

Movie Theater Popcorn

Ingredients:

¼ cup coconut oil

1 cup popcorn

⅓ cup unsalted butter, melted

1 teaspoon popcorn salt

1. Pour oil into wok and set to SEAR.
2. Add popcorn to wok; cover.
3. Let popcorn pop until popping slows to a pop per second.
4. Transfer popcorn to a bowl.
5. Drizzle popcorn with melted butter and sprinkle with popcorn salt.

Toffee Nut Crunch

Ingredients:

Butter-flavored non-stick cooking spray

Parchment paper

1 cup unsalted butter

1 cup sugar

4 tablespoons water

2 tablespoons corn syrup

12 ounces milk chocolate, finely chopped

1 cup slivered almonds, chopped

1. Line a jelly roll pan with parchment paper.
2. Apply non-stick spray to parchment paper.
3. Add butter, sugar, water and corn syrup to wok; mix well.
4. Set wok to SEAR.
5. Using a candy thermometer, measure temperature until it reaches 290 degrees.
6. Pour mixture into jelly roll pan; spread evenly using a rubber spatula.
7. Sprinkle with chocolate and let melt.
8. Top with chopped almonds and refrigerate for 20 minutes.
9. Break into pieces and serve.

Peaches In Champagne Syrup

Ingredients:

½ cup water

½ cup champagne

¾ cup sugar

1 vanilla bean, split

6 peaches, pitted and quartered

Vanilla ice cream

1. Add water, champagne, sugar and vanilla bean to wok.
2. Set wok to SEAR and simmer for 3 minutes.
3. Using a fork, pierce peaches while leaving the skin on.
4. Place peaches into wok; simmer for 5 minutes.
5. Serve hot or cold over vanilla ice cream.

Deb's Tip:
Instead of peaches, try using plums or apricots.

Bananas Foster

Makes 4 servings

Ingredients:

½ cup unsalted butter

½ cup brown sugar

4 ripe bananas, cut into 2-inch pieces

¼ teaspoon ground cinnamon

2 tablespoons banana liqueur

¼ cup spiced rum

Vanilla ice cream

1. Set wok to MEDIUM.
2. Add butter to wok; let melt.
3. Add brown sugar to wok; stir.
4. Add bananas to wok; cook for 2 minutes.
5. Increase wok to HIGH.
6. Add cinnamon, liqueur and rum to wok; stir.
7. Serve over vanilla ice cream.

Pumpkin Fudge

Ingredients:

Non-stick cooking spray

½ cup unsalted butter

2 cups sugar

½ cup evaporated milk

1 tablespoon corn syrup

¼ cup pumpkin puree

1 teaspoon pumpkin pie spice

1 cup butterscotch morsels

1 cup marshmallow cream

½ cup walnuts, chopped

1. Spray a 9 X 9 inch baking pan with non-stick spray.
2. Set wok to MEDIUM.
3. Add butter to wok and let melt.
4. Add sugar, milk, syrup, puree and pumpkin spice to wok; mix well.
5. Increase wok to SEAR.
6. Using a candy thermometer, measure temperature until it reaches 240 degrees.
7. Turn off wok and add remaining ingredients.
8. Pour mixture into prepared pan.
9. Let rest for 2 hours, cut into squares and serve.

Peanut Brittle

Ingredients:

Parchment paper

Butter-flavored non-stick spray

1 cup sugar

1 cup light corn syrup

1 tablespoon unsalted butter

2 cups dry roasted peanuts

1 tablespoon baking soda

1 teaspoon vanilla

1. Line a jelly roll pan with parchment paper.
2. Apply non-stick spray to parchment paper.
3. Add sugar, corn syrup, butter and peanuts to wok; stir well.
4. Set wok to SEAR.
5. Using a candy thermometer, measure temperature until it reaches 295 degrees; do not stir.
6. Turn off wok.
7. Add baking soda and vanilla to wok; stir.
8. Pour mixture into pan and spread evenly using a rubber spatula.
9. Let cool completely.
10. Break brittle into pieces and serve.

Deb's Tip:
Try chopped macadamia or pistachio nuts instead of peanuts.

Old Fashioned Candy Apples

Ingredients:

8 apples

Parchment paper

8 lollipop sticks

2 cups sugar

¾ cup water

½ cup light corn syrup

½ teaspoon red food coloring

4 drops cinnamon extract

1. Wash and dry apples.
2. Line a cookie sheet with parchment paper.
3. Insert a lollipop stick into the stem end of each apple.
4. Add sugar, water and corn syrup to wok; mix well.
5. Set wok to SEAR.
6. Using a candy thermometer, measure temperature until it reaches 290 degrees; turn off wok.
7. Add food coloring and cinnamon extract to wok; mix well.
8. Rotate apples into candy mixture until completely covered.
9. Place apples on cookie sheet and let cool.

Deb's Tip:
To mix it up, try using different kinds of food coloring and extracts.

Index

Index

Index

Index

Index

Sausage

Seafood

Shrimp

Soups

Stir-Frys

T

V

Index

Vegetables

W

Y

Z

For more of Deb's delicious
ideas, please visit:
www.cookingwithdeb.com